OLYMPIAD WORKBOOK

INTERNATIONAL ENGLISH OLYMPIAD

AF344951

- **01** Learning Objectives
- **02** Multiple Choice Questions
- **03** HOTS (Achievers Section)
- **04** Model Test Paper
- **05** Answer Keys and Solutions
- **06** OMR Answer Sheet

V&S PUBLISHERS

Published by:

V&S PUBLISHERS

F-2/16, Ansari road, Daryaganj, New Delhi-110002
☎ 23240026, 23240027 • *Fax:* 011-23240028
✉ info@vspublishers.com • 🌐 www.vspublishers.com

 **Online Brandstore: amazon.in/vspublishers**

Regional Office : Hyderabad
5-1-707/1, Brij Bhawan (Beside Central Bank of India Lane)
Bank Street, Koti, Hyderabad - 500 095
☎ 040-24737290
✉ vspublishershyd@gmail.com

Follow us on:   

BUY OUR BOOKS FROM: | AMAZON | | FLIPKART |

DISCLAIMER

While every attempt has been made to provide accurate and timely information in this book, neither the author nor the publisher assumes any responsibility for errors, unintended omissions or commissions detected therein. The author and publisher makes no representation or warranty with respect to the comprehensiveness or completeness of the contents provided.

All matters included have been simplified under professional guidance for general information only, without any warranty for applicability on an individual. Any mention of an organization or a website in the book, by way of citation or as a source of additional information, doesn't imply the endorsement of the content either by the author or the publisher. It is possible that websites cited may have changed or removed between the time of editing and publishing the book.

Results from using the expert opinion in this book will be totally dependent on individual circumstances and factors beyond the control of the author and the publisher.

It makes sense to elicit advice from well informed sources before implementing the ideas given in the book. The reader assumes full responsibility for the consequences arising out from reading this book.

For proper guidance, it is advisable to read the book under the watchful eyes of parents/guardian. The buyer of this book assumes all responsibility for the use of given materials and information.

The copyright of the entire content of this book rests with the author/publisher. Any infringement/transmission of the cover design, text or illustrations, in any form, by any means, by any entity will invite legal action and be responsible for consequences thereon.

PUBLISHER'S NOTE

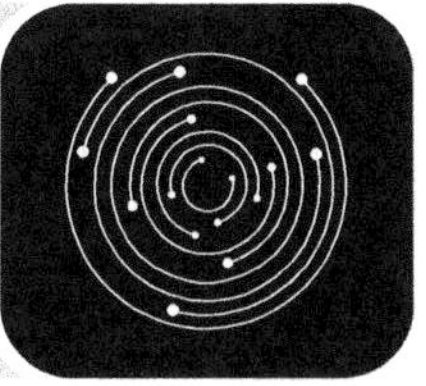

V&S Publishers has carved a significant niche in the publishing industry over the last decade, having successfully published more than 1000 titles across 9 languages spanning over 50 subject categories. Being known for the quality of content, we have built a reputation of excellence and reliability. We have consistently delivered **"Value & Substance"** to our readers, through a wide range of titles across a variety of genres covering school books, fiction and non-fiction that caters to different people from every section of the society.

The **Olympiad Guidebooks for classes 1-10** across all subjects, launched almost a decade ago, under the **GEN X Imprint**, became a go-to-source for the school students in no time, owing to their invaluable and substantive content written in a guidebook pattern,.

Having successfully sold a million copies of the same and in response to demand by both students as well as shopkeepers nationwide; we now present before you our newly launched **Olympiad Workbook Series**, designed for **classes 1-10 across 4 subjects**.

The workbooks are meticulously curated by a team of experienced educators, researchers and subject matter experts, edited by professionals and peer reviewed by teachers. The team has poured its efforts and expertise into creating a crisp and concise workbook which will help and guide the students to the path of success in Olympiad exams. The **MCQs** identified will not only help in scoring top marks in Olympiads but also inculcate a sense of deeper understanding of the subject, by way of solving **HOTS** and referring to complete solutions at the end of the book.

Here we present our new release– **OLYMPIAD WORKBOOK (IEO) CLASS–4** having following features:

- ☞ Based on the latest syllabi
- ☞ MCQs with comprehensive coverage of topics
- ☞ HOTS Questions liberally included
- ☞ A dedicated chapter on logical reasoning
- ☞ Model test paper for thorough practice
- ☞ Sample OMR sheet for real time simulation

We have made sure through our best efforts, that this workbook strictly follows the latest syllabi and patterns of the Olympiad Examination.

As **V&S Publishers** continuously strive to enhance the readability and maintain the credibility of our academic publications, we seek the support of our valuable readers in influencing and enriching the lives of future generations of students.

P.S. While every care has been taken to ensure the correctness of the content, if you come across any error, howsoever minor, do not hesitate to discuss with teachers while pointing that out to us in no uncertain terms.

We wish you all the best for your exams!

DISTINCTIVE FEATURES

01 Learning Objectives

They list the whole chapter as subtopics, helping the teachers to guide children in a step-by-step manner.

02 Multiple Choice Questions

MCQs act as an excellent learning aid, helping you to understand and work on your mistakes.

03 HOTS (Achievers Section)

The High Order Thinking Questions aim to help the student to solve Application-based questions and gain practical understanding of the subject.

04 Model Test Paper

Model test paper are provided at the end of each book, which help the student to test the knowledge which they have gained after thorough reading of all chapters.

05 Answer Key

Detailed Answer Key along with explanations aid the pupil to indentify, understand the mistakes they make during the course of Olympiad preparation.

CONTENTS

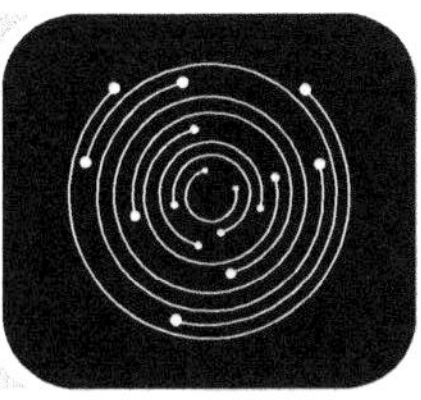

VOCABULARY

LEARNING OBJECTIVES

➤ Write spellings of some common words

➤ Concept of Collocation

➤ Animals and their types

➤ Household items

➤ Different emotions

PRACTICE EXERCISE

I. Pick the correct option for the following sentences

1. My uncle is a priest/preist.

2. The name of the qween/queen of England is Elizabeth.

3. I have just one box here, the rest of the boxes are in the other room.

4. We should give your mother the correct information. She should not be misinformed/misenformed.

5. Do you want to drive? Sure, I like driving/driveing.

6. It nearly midnight. Allmost/almost your birthday.

7. There was a robbery in the club last night. The theif/thief took all the electronics.

8. Can you supply the food tomorrow? Can you have it supplied/supplyed by 4:00 pm.

9. Do you want to play TT? No thanks, I played/plaid this morning.

10. I am aware of the class time table. I am unaware/unawair of the date of the exam.

II. What can the following items be categorised as?

11. Sharpeners : _____________

12. Plates : _____________

13. Turmeric : _____________

14. Socks : _____________

15. Lotion : _____________

16. Pans : _____________

17. Salt : _____________

18. Stapler : _____________

19. Frock : _____________

10. Nutmeg : _____________

III. Place the following emotions under the correct head out of the 8 major emotions discussed in the chapter: See the example.

Jealousy : Envy

21. Caring : _____________

22. Hate : _____________

23. Fright : _____________

24. Likeness : _____________

25. Remorsefulness : _____________

26. Rage : _____________

27. Grief : _____________

28. Astonishment : _____________

29. Alarm : ________________
30. Empathy : ________________
31. Fury : ________________
32. Gloom : ________________

33. Amazement : ________________
34. Guilty : ________________
35. Terror : ________________

HOTS (ACHIEVERS SECTION)

IV. Form the correct questions for the following answers:

36. Yes, I love Marathi food.

37. My roll number is 38.

V. Pick out five correct answers for all of the following places where you find animals:

38. **Farm:** Dogs, camels, antelopes, sheep, horses, whales, cows, bison, chicken.

39. **City roads:** Wild cats, squirrels, bears, foxes, cows, tigers, dogs, pigeons, goldfish, goats.

VI. Select the correct option from the ones given for each emotion.

40. Woe
   (A) Love   (B) Envy
   (C) Sadness   (D) Shame

1.	Ⓐ Ⓑ Ⓒ Ⓓ	9.	Ⓐ Ⓑ Ⓒ Ⓓ	17.	Ⓐ Ⓑ Ⓒ Ⓓ	25.	Ⓐ Ⓑ Ⓒ Ⓓ	33.	Ⓐ Ⓑ Ⓒ Ⓓ
2.	Ⓐ Ⓑ Ⓒ Ⓓ	10.	Ⓐ Ⓑ Ⓒ Ⓓ	18.	Ⓐ Ⓑ Ⓒ Ⓓ	26.	Ⓐ Ⓑ Ⓒ Ⓓ	34.	Ⓐ Ⓑ Ⓒ Ⓓ
3.	Ⓐ Ⓑ Ⓒ Ⓓ	11.	Ⓐ Ⓑ Ⓒ Ⓓ	19.	Ⓐ Ⓑ Ⓒ Ⓓ	27.	Ⓐ Ⓑ Ⓒ Ⓓ	35.	Ⓐ Ⓑ Ⓒ Ⓓ
4.	Ⓐ Ⓑ Ⓒ Ⓓ	12.	Ⓐ Ⓑ Ⓒ Ⓓ	20.	Ⓐ Ⓑ Ⓒ Ⓓ	28.	Ⓐ Ⓑ Ⓒ Ⓓ	36.	Ⓐ Ⓑ Ⓒ Ⓓ
5.	Ⓐ Ⓑ Ⓒ Ⓓ	13.	Ⓐ Ⓑ Ⓒ Ⓓ	21.	Ⓐ Ⓑ Ⓒ Ⓓ	29.	Ⓐ Ⓑ Ⓒ Ⓓ	37.	Ⓐ Ⓑ Ⓒ Ⓓ
6.	Ⓐ Ⓑ Ⓒ Ⓓ	14.	Ⓐ Ⓑ Ⓒ Ⓓ	22.	Ⓐ Ⓑ Ⓒ Ⓓ	30.	Ⓐ Ⓑ Ⓒ Ⓓ	38.	Ⓐ Ⓑ Ⓒ Ⓓ
7.	Ⓐ Ⓑ Ⓒ Ⓓ	15.	Ⓐ Ⓑ Ⓒ Ⓓ	23.	Ⓐ Ⓑ Ⓒ Ⓓ	31.	Ⓐ Ⓑ Ⓒ Ⓓ	39.	Ⓐ Ⓑ Ⓒ Ⓓ
8.	Ⓐ Ⓑ Ⓒ Ⓓ	16.	Ⓐ Ⓑ Ⓒ Ⓓ	24.	Ⓐ Ⓑ Ⓒ Ⓓ	32.	Ⓐ Ⓑ Ⓒ Ⓓ	40.	Ⓐ Ⓑ Ⓒ Ⓓ

SYNONYMS AND ANTONYMS 

LEARNING OBJECTIVES

➤ Some common synonyms
➤ Some common antonyms

PRACTICE EXERCISE

I. Select the correct synonym of the word given in capital letter in each question.

1. ACCURATE
   - (A) Correct
   - (B) Incorrect
   - (C) Wrong
   - (D) Possible

2. ADMIRE
   - (A) Praise
   - (B) Allow
   - (C) Obey
   - (D) Play

3. ANNUAL
   - (A) Weekly
   - (B) Daily
   - (C) Monthly
   - (D) Yearly

4. BEGIN
   - (A) Close
   - (B) Stop
   - (C) Start
   - (D) End

5. ANGER
   - (A) Happiness
   - (B) Pleasure
   - (C) Joy
   - (D) Wrath

6. ASSEMBLY
   - (A) House
   - (B) Building
   - (C) Hut
   - (D) Gathering

7. CONVERSATION
   - (A) Sing
   - (B) Talk
   - (C) Dance
   - (D) Walk

8. SEARCH
   - (A) Find
   - (B) Loose
   - (C) Lost
   - (D) Look

9. UNITE
   - (A) Divide
   - (B) Separate
   - (C) Part
   - (D) Join

10. WEALTHY
    - (A) Poor
    - (B) Hungry
    - (C) Miserable
    - (D) Rich

11. MIDDLE
    - (A) Corner
    - (B) Centre
    - (C) End
    - (D) Beginning

12. ERROR
    - (A) Mistake
    - (B) Strong
    - (C) Powerful
    - (D) Healthy

13. FORTUNATE
    - (A) Unlucky
    - (B) Failed
    - (C) Lucky
    - (D) Unsuccessful

14. GENEROUS
    - (A) Kind
    - (B) Mean
    - (C) Cruel
    - (D) Unpleasant

15. ORDINARY
    - (A) Expensive
    - (B) Rare
    - (C) Common
    - (D) Unusual

16. FOOLISH
    - (A) Intelligent
    - (B) Clever
    - (C) Silly
    - (D) Smart

17. REPLY
    (A) Answer
    (B) Ask
    (C) Question
    (D) Interrogate
18. FOE
    (A) Enemy
    (B) Well wisher
    (C) Friend
    (D) Pal
19. ODOUR
    (A) Order
    (B) Smell
    (C) Colour
    (D) Taste
20. STORY
    (A) Tale
    (B) Write
    (C) Start
    (D) Funny

II. Select the correct antonym of the word given in capital letter.

21. ACCEPT
    (A) Reject
    (B) Agree
    (C) Tiny
    (D) Regard
22. AGREE
    (A) Disagree
    (B) Defend
    (C) Worse
    (D) Tight
23. ABSENT
    (A) Lost
    (B) Found
    (C) Choose
    (D) Present
24. ANCIENT
    (A) Old
    (B) Very old
    (C) Early
    (D) Modern
25. ATTACK
    (A) Defend
    (B) Damage
    (C) Hurt
    (D) Harm
26. BOTTOM
    (A) Top
    (B) Base
    (C) Floor
    (D) Foot
27. BLUNT
    (A) Dull
    (B) Rounded
    (C) Honest
    (D) Sharp
28. EMPTY
    (A) Blank
    (B) Full
    (C) Bare
    (D) Vacant
29. COARSE
    (A) Rough
    (B) Uneven
    (C) Harsh
    (D) Fine
30. DANGEROUS
    (A) Unsafe
    (B) Risky
    (C) Hazardous
    (D) Safe

Choose the correct synonym of the word given in CAPITAL LETTERS.

31. ANGRY
    (A) Calm   (B) Tranquil
    (C) Annoyed   (D) Quite
    (E) Cool

32. FRANK
    (A) Bold   (B) Good
    (C) Bad   (D) Beautiful
    (E) Ugly

33. LAZY
    (A) Indolent   (B) Fall
    (C) Right   (D) Trash
    (E) Sharp

34. OVERCOME
    (A) Prominent   (B) Defeat
    (C) Bandit   (D) Get
    (E) None of these

35. POLITE
    (A) Civil   (B) Danger
    (C) Endless   (D) Excuse
    (E) None of these

— Darken Your Choice with HB Pencil —

1.	Ⓐ Ⓑ Ⓒ Ⓓ	8.	Ⓐ Ⓑ Ⓒ Ⓓ	15.	Ⓐ Ⓑ Ⓒ Ⓓ	22	Ⓐ Ⓑ Ⓒ Ⓓ	29.	Ⓐ Ⓑ Ⓒ Ⓓ
2.	Ⓐ Ⓑ Ⓒ Ⓓ	9.	Ⓐ Ⓑ Ⓒ Ⓓ	16.	Ⓐ Ⓑ Ⓒ Ⓓ	23.	Ⓐ Ⓑ Ⓒ Ⓓ	30.	Ⓐ Ⓑ Ⓒ Ⓓ
3.	Ⓐ Ⓑ Ⓒ Ⓓ	10.	Ⓐ Ⓑ Ⓒ Ⓓ	17.	Ⓐ Ⓑ Ⓒ Ⓓ	24.	Ⓐ Ⓑ Ⓒ Ⓓ	31.	Ⓐ Ⓑ Ⓒ Ⓓ
4.	Ⓐ Ⓑ Ⓒ Ⓓ	11.	Ⓐ Ⓑ Ⓒ Ⓓ	18.	Ⓐ Ⓑ Ⓒ Ⓓ	25.	Ⓐ Ⓑ Ⓒ Ⓓ	32.	Ⓐ Ⓑ Ⓒ Ⓓ
5.	Ⓐ Ⓑ Ⓒ Ⓓ	12.	Ⓐ Ⓑ Ⓒ Ⓓ	19.	Ⓐ Ⓑ Ⓒ Ⓓ	26.	Ⓐ Ⓑ Ⓒ Ⓓ	33.	Ⓐ Ⓑ Ⓒ Ⓓ
6.	Ⓐ Ⓑ Ⓒ Ⓓ	13.	Ⓐ Ⓑ Ⓒ Ⓓ	20.	Ⓐ Ⓑ Ⓒ Ⓓ	27.	Ⓐ Ⓑ Ⓒ Ⓓ	34.	Ⓐ Ⓑ Ⓒ Ⓓ
7.	Ⓐ Ⓑ Ⓒ Ⓓ	14.	Ⓐ Ⓑ Ⓒ Ⓓ	21.	Ⓐ Ⓑ Ⓒ Ⓓ	28.	Ⓐ Ⓑ Ⓒ Ⓓ	35.	Ⓐ Ⓑ Ⓒ Ⓓ

NOUNS AND PRONOUNS

LEARNING OBJECTIVES

➤ Nouns and their types

➤ Pronouns and their types

PRACTICE EXERCISE

I. **Find out the kind of noun the underlined word has from the given options.**

1. She had <u>pain</u> in her legs.
   (A) Abstract noun
   (B) Common noun
   (C) Collective noun
   (D) Material noun

2. Most of the <u>doctors</u> in our country avoid serving in rural areas.
   (A) Proper noun
   (B) Collective noun
   (C) Common noun
   (D) Material noun

3. Elephants more often move in <u>herd</u>.
   (A) Proper noun
   (B) Common noun
   (C) Material noun
   (D) Collective noun

4. <u>Students</u> sit together in the class.
   (A) Collective noun
   (B) Common noun
   (C) Proper noun
   (D) Material noun

5. <u>New York</u> is a beautiful city.
   (A) Collective noun
   (B) Common noun
   (C) Proper noun
   (D) Material noun

6. The man is known for his <u>wisdom</u>.
   (A) Proper noun
   (B) Collective noun
   (C) Material noun
   (D) Abstract noun

7. The commercial capital of India is <u>Mumbai</u>.
   (A) Common noun
   (B) Collective noun
   (C) Proper noun
   (D) Material noun

8. A <u>pair</u> of shoes
   (A) Proper noun
   (B) Common noun
   (C) Collective noun
   (D) Material noun

9. A <u>team</u> of players
   (A) Proper noun
   (B) Common noun
   (C) Material noun
   (D) Collective noun

10. The <u>length</u> of this room is four metres.
    (A) Abstract noun
    (B) Collective noun
    (C) Proper noun
    (D) Material noun

11. <u>Ram</u> is going to the market.
    (A) Proper noun

(B) Common noun
(C) Collective noun
(D) Abstract noun

12. Sita went to the garden and studied a <u>flock of birds</u>.
(A) Proper noun
(B) Common noun
(C) Collective noun
(D) Abstract noun

13. The women went to see the <u>butterflies</u>.
(A) Proper noun
(B) Common noun
(C) Collective noun
(D) Abstract noun

14. Thomas Edison invented the <u>light bulb</u>.
(A) Proper noun
(B) Common noun
(C) Collective noun
(D) Abstract noun

15. <u>Birbal</u> was Emperor Akbar's favourite minister.
(A) Proper noun
(B) Common noun
(C) Collective noun
(D) Abstract noun

II. Use the correct form of pronoun to complete the following sentences:

16. _______________ is a pronoun? It is a word which is used in the place of a noun. (interrogative)
(A) Who
(B) It
(C) Them
(D) What

17. Priya wants to paint __________ room pink. (possessive)
(A) Them
(B) Herself
(C) Her
(D) Who

18. _______________ people come here to shop even in early morning. (Indefinite)
(A) Her
(B) Some
(C) Any
(D) Everybody

19. _______________ can still go to the playground, it's just 7pm. (Personal)
(A) Each
(B) Anybody
(C) It
(D) You

20. _______________ of the trains will do. I just need to get to Srinagar. (Distributive)
(A) Any
(B) Himself
(C) Each other
(D) Those

21. I like those clothes __________ have pockets. (relative)
(A) Themselves
(B) I
(C) Who
(D) Which

22. Saumya has hurt _____________. (Reflexive)
(A) Herself
(B) It
(C) Which
(D) That

23. This book is _______________. I bought it in Shimla. (possessive)
(A) It
(B) Mine
(C) His
(D) They

24. This is the house _____________ I was talking about. (Relative)
(A) Itself
(B) Who
(C) Whose
(D) Which

25. Don't worry so much this time __________ will definitely be selected for the team. (Personal)
(A) You
(B) Who
(C) Which
(D) That

26. _____________ has called back from the shop. I am still waiting. (Indefinite)
(A) Few
(B) Nobody
(C) Itself
(D) Which

27. Is __________ the movie you were talking about? (Demonstrative)
(A) Which
(B) They
(C) That
(D) My

28. _______________ must be careful while one is crossing the road. (indefinite)

(A) Myself   (B) One

(C) It   (D) I

29. I will _____________ lock up the shop. (emphatic)

(A) Itself   (B) Themselves

(C) Myself   (D) Yourself

30. _____________ knows the correct answer? (interrogative)

(A) Who

(B) I

(C) That

(D) Which

HOTS (ACHIEVERS SECTION)

Fill in the blanks with appropriate noun:

31. There was no _____ among the rotten apples.

(A) kind   (B) beauty

(C) fresh   (D) choice

32. There is a cut throat _______ in every trade.

(A) market   (B) choice

(C) competition   (D) familiarity

33. A ____ of people gathered at the meeting.

(A) flight   (B) herd

(C) crowd   (D) swarm

Choose the pronoun in each statement and choose under which variety does it fall into.

34. I thought you knew him.

(A) Demonstrative   (B) Personal

(C) Possessive   (D) Reflexive

35. These books are ours.

(A) Demonstrative   (B) Personal

(C) Possessive   (D) Reflexive

Darken Your Choice with HB Pencil

1.	Ⓐ Ⓑ Ⓒ Ⓓ	8.	Ⓐ Ⓑ Ⓒ Ⓓ	15.	Ⓐ Ⓑ Ⓒ Ⓓ	22	Ⓐ Ⓑ Ⓒ Ⓓ	29.	Ⓐ Ⓑ Ⓒ Ⓓ
2.	Ⓐ Ⓑ Ⓒ Ⓓ	9.	Ⓐ Ⓑ Ⓒ Ⓓ	16.	Ⓐ Ⓑ Ⓒ Ⓓ	23.	Ⓐ Ⓑ Ⓒ Ⓓ	30.	Ⓐ Ⓑ Ⓒ Ⓓ
3.	Ⓐ Ⓑ Ⓒ Ⓓ	10.	Ⓐ Ⓑ Ⓒ Ⓓ	17.	Ⓐ Ⓑ Ⓒ Ⓓ	24.	Ⓐ Ⓑ Ⓒ Ⓓ	31.	Ⓐ Ⓑ Ⓒ Ⓓ
4.	Ⓐ Ⓑ Ⓒ Ⓓ	11.	Ⓐ Ⓑ Ⓒ Ⓓ	18.	Ⓐ Ⓑ Ⓒ Ⓓ	25.	Ⓐ Ⓑ Ⓒ Ⓓ	32.	Ⓐ Ⓑ Ⓒ Ⓓ
5.	Ⓐ Ⓑ Ⓒ Ⓓ	12.	Ⓐ Ⓑ Ⓒ Ⓓ	19.	Ⓐ Ⓑ Ⓒ Ⓓ	26.	Ⓐ Ⓑ Ⓒ Ⓓ	33.	Ⓐ Ⓑ Ⓒ Ⓓ
6.	Ⓐ Ⓑ Ⓒ Ⓓ	13.	Ⓐ Ⓑ Ⓒ Ⓓ	20.	Ⓐ Ⓑ Ⓒ Ⓓ	27.	Ⓐ Ⓑ Ⓒ Ⓓ	34.	Ⓐ Ⓑ Ⓒ Ⓓ
7.	Ⓐ Ⓑ Ⓒ Ⓓ	14.	Ⓐ Ⓑ Ⓒ Ⓓ	21.	Ⓐ Ⓑ Ⓒ Ⓓ	28.	Ⓐ Ⓑ Ⓒ Ⓓ	35.	Ⓐ Ⓑ Ⓒ Ⓓ

VERBS

LEARNING OBJECTIVES

➤ Verbs and their different types

PRACTICE EXERCISE

I. Rewrite each of the sentences using the correct form of the irregular verb

1. I went to the concert, she sing very well. (past participle)

   Answer: _______________________________

2. The guitar I bought last week cost me rupees 4000. (past tense)

   Answer: _______________________________

3. Who win the tennis match last evening? (past tense)

   Answer: _______________________________

4. Have you see my phone? I can't find it. (past participle)

   Answer: _______________________________

5. The bird fly over us before settling down on a tree branch. (past tense)

   Answer: _______________________________

6. Dad become angry when he heard that we had left the TV on all night. (past tense)

   Answer: _______________________________

7. Have you cut the cake already? We are reaching in ten minutes! (past participle)

   Answer: _______________________________

8. When was this email write? Check the time. (past participle)

   Answer: _______________________________

9. When was the Qutub Minar build? (past tense)

   Answer: _______________________________

10. From all the boys in the team, Aditya was choose to represent the school. (past participle)

    Answer: _______________________________

11. I give the chocolates to Nikhil as soon as I see him. (past tense, past tense)

    Answer: _______________________________

12. We spend the whole evening eating pop corn and chocolates. (post tense)

    Answer: _______________________________

13. I told her the whole incident in detail and I think she understand. (past tense)

    Answer: _______________________________

14. Who took my watch from the table? It was take by Anand. (past participle)

Answer: _______________________________

____

15. I was telling her the movie's story but she already know it all. (past tense)

Answer: _______________________________

____

II. Choose the correct option to complete the sentence

16. Sumit showed/shown me the birthday pictures.

17. Have you ate/eaten your dinner?

18. My new tee shirt has shrunk/shrank after washing.

19. There were strawberry ice cream and chocolate ice cream. I chosen/chose chocolate.

20. By the time we reached the house, the maid was go/gone.

21. It's a beautiful guitar and it costeds/costs only 3000 rupees.

22. I meets/met Richa at Mayank's birthday party.

23. I heard/hear them practicing all of last evening.

24. The ticket was tear/torn but the ticket-checker let us in.

25. The batsman was catch/caught behind the wickets and Australia lost the match.

HOTS (ACHIEVERS SECTION)

Complete the following sentences using the correct form of the irregular verb:

26. He _______________ 2 hours just to get the tickets.

    (A) Spends   (B) Spent
    (C) Spend   (D) Spending

27. Shweta _________ a new purse last week.

    (A) Get   (B) Getting
    (C) Gets   (D) Got

28. We last _______________ at Shalu's birthday party.

    (A) Met   (B) Meet
    (C) Meeting   (D) Mets

29. By the time we reached the mall, everyone was already _________

    (A) See   (B) Go
    (C) Gone   (D) Going

30. I already _________ when Natasha was coming but, I still called to confirm.

    (A) Knowing   (B) Knew
    (C) Know   (D) Knows

—Darken Your Choice with HB Pencil—

1.	Ⓐ Ⓑ Ⓒ Ⓓ	7.	Ⓐ Ⓑ Ⓒ Ⓓ	13.	Ⓐ Ⓑ Ⓒ Ⓓ	19	Ⓐ Ⓑ Ⓒ Ⓓ	25.	Ⓐ Ⓑ Ⓒ Ⓓ
2.	Ⓐ Ⓑ Ⓒ Ⓓ	8.	Ⓐ Ⓑ Ⓒ Ⓓ	14.	Ⓐ Ⓑ Ⓒ Ⓓ	20.	Ⓐ Ⓑ Ⓒ Ⓓ	26.	Ⓐ Ⓑ Ⓒ Ⓓ
3.	Ⓐ Ⓑ Ⓒ Ⓓ	9.	Ⓐ Ⓑ Ⓒ Ⓓ	15.	Ⓐ Ⓑ Ⓒ Ⓓ	21.	Ⓐ Ⓑ Ⓒ Ⓓ	27.	Ⓐ Ⓑ Ⓒ Ⓓ
4.	Ⓐ Ⓑ Ⓒ Ⓓ	10.	Ⓐ Ⓑ Ⓒ Ⓓ	16.	Ⓐ Ⓑ Ⓒ Ⓓ	22.	Ⓐ Ⓑ Ⓒ Ⓓ	28.	Ⓐ Ⓑ Ⓒ Ⓓ
5.	Ⓐ Ⓑ Ⓒ Ⓓ	11.	Ⓐ Ⓑ Ⓒ Ⓓ	17.	Ⓐ Ⓑ Ⓒ Ⓓ	23.	Ⓐ Ⓑ Ⓒ Ⓓ	29.	Ⓐ Ⓑ Ⓒ Ⓓ
6.	Ⓐ Ⓑ Ⓒ Ⓓ	12.	Ⓐ Ⓑ Ⓒ Ⓓ	18.	Ⓐ Ⓑ Ⓒ Ⓓ	24.	Ⓐ Ⓑ Ⓒ Ⓓ	30.	Ⓐ Ⓑ Ⓒ Ⓓ

OLYMPIAD WORKBOOK (IEO) CLASS— 4

ADVERBS AND ADJECTIVES 

LEARNING OBJECTIVES

➤ Different types of adverbs

➤ Different types of adjectives

PRACTICE EXERCISE

I. Read the following sentences and fill in the blanks with one of the options given below.

1. _________ does the team meet for cricket practice? We meet every Sunday at *7 am*
   (A) Where (place)
   (B) When (time)
   (C) How (manner)
   (D) How often (time)

2. _____________do I open this box? There is a latch on the other side.
   (A) When (time)
   (B) How often (time)
   (C) Where (place)
   (D) How (manner)

3. _________ does this dress cost? It costs rupess 3000.
   (A) How much (quantity)
   (B) Where (place)
   (C) How long (time)
   (D) When (time)

4. __________ do you want to have dinner? Let's go to McDonald's?
   (A) How much (quantity)
   (B) Where (place)
   (C) How long (time)
   (D) How (manner)

5. _____________ will you get the result? Tomorrow, I think.

   (A) How often (number)
   (B) Why (cause and effect)
   (C) Where (place)
   (D) When (time)

6. _____________is your mother doing now? She is much better after taking the medicines.
   (A) How (manner)
   (B) How (condition)
   (C) How many (number)
   (D) How much (degree)

7. _____________ is she staying this time? She is staying in Jaisalmer.
   (A) How many (number)
   (B) Where (place)
   (C) Are (condition)
   (D) When (time)

8. _____________ is her wedding? It is day after tomorrow.
   (A) How often (number)
   (B) Where (place)
   (C) How much (degree)
   (D) When (time)

9. _______________ gifts did she get on her birthday? She got almost 30 gifts!
   (A) Where (place)
   (B) How often (number)
   (C) How many (number)
   (D) How much (degree)

10. I understand that you like the movie but
________________ times can you watch it!
(A) How many (number)
(B) Where (place)
(C) How (manner)
(D) How often (number)

II. Choose the correct option and fill in the blanks.

11. We saw __________ animals at the zoo.
(A) much   (B) many
(C) Both (A) and (B)   (D) none of these

12. How __________ oranges did you put in the box?
(A) much   (B) many
(C) Both (A) and (B)   (D) none of these

13. There isn't __________ sugar in my coffee.
(A) much   (B) many
(C) Both a and b   (D) none of these

14. I don't have __________ friends.
(A) much   (B) many
(C) Both (A) and (B)   (D) none of these

15. The old man hasn't got ______ hair on his head.
(A) much   (B) many
(C) Both (A) and (B)   (D) none of these

16. I've packed __________ bottles of water.
(A) much   (B) many
(C) Both (A) and (B)   (D) none of these

17. I didn't get __________ sleep last night.
(A) much   (B) many
(C) Both (A) and (B)   (D) none of these

18. How __________ fruit do you eat everyday?
(A) much   (B) many
(C) Both (A) and (B)   (D) none of these

19. Can you please buy __________ apples?
(A) a few   (B) a little
(C) Both (A) and (B)   (D) none of these

20. We need ________ water.
(A) a few   (B) a little
(C) Both (A) and (B)   (D) none of these

21. I have ________ money left.
(A) a few   (B) a little
(C) Both (A) and (B)   (D) none of these

22. I take ________ sugar with my coffee.
(A) a few   (B) a little
(C) Both (A) and (B)   (D) none of these

23. We had ________ pints of beer there.
(A) a few   (B) a little
(C) Both (A) and (B)   (D) none of these

24. You have ________ time left.
(A) a few   (B) a little
(C) Both (A) and (B)   (D) none of these

25. There are ________ chairs in the room.
(A) a few   (B) a little
(C) Both (A) and (B)   (D) none of these

26. He only spent ________ dollars there.
(A) a few   (B) a little
(C) Both (A) and (B)   (D) none of these

27. I have ________ interest in classical music.
(A) Little   (B) Less
(C) Both (A) and (B)   (D) None of these

28. I have ________ faith in him.
(A) little   (B) less
(C) Both (A) and (B)   (D) none of these

29. We need ________ furniture in this dance hall than in the big one.
(A) little   (B) less
(C) Both (A) and (B)   (D) None of these

30. You have to drink __________ coffee.
(A) little
(B) less
(C) Both (A) and (B)
(D) none of these

Form the correct sentences based on the hints given in brackets with each sentence.

31. The class begins at 11/on the high-way. (adverb of time)

32. The Rhino lives in strong/Assam. (adverb of place)

33. I partially agree/stupidly that we should call him right away! (adverb of affirmation and negation)

34. An adjective of quality describes the ___________ of a noun.
   (A) characteristics   (B) quantity
   (C) output   (D) none of these

35. We use an interrogative adjective to
   (A) ask question   (B) point
   (C) characteristics   (D) none of these

—Darken Your Choice with HB Pencil—

1.	Ⓐ Ⓑ Ⓒ Ⓓ	8.	Ⓐ Ⓑ Ⓒ Ⓓ	15.	Ⓐ Ⓑ Ⓒ Ⓓ	22	Ⓐ Ⓑ Ⓒ Ⓓ	29.	Ⓐ Ⓑ Ⓒ Ⓓ
2.	Ⓐ Ⓑ Ⓒ Ⓓ	9.	Ⓐ Ⓑ Ⓒ Ⓓ	16.	Ⓐ Ⓑ Ⓒ Ⓓ	23.	Ⓐ Ⓑ Ⓒ Ⓓ	30.	Ⓐ Ⓑ Ⓒ Ⓓ
3.	Ⓐ Ⓑ Ⓒ Ⓓ	10.	Ⓐ Ⓑ Ⓒ Ⓓ	17.	Ⓐ Ⓑ Ⓒ Ⓓ	24.	Ⓐ Ⓑ Ⓒ Ⓓ	31.	Ⓐ Ⓑ Ⓒ Ⓓ
4.	Ⓐ Ⓑ Ⓒ Ⓓ	11.	Ⓐ Ⓑ Ⓒ Ⓓ	18.	Ⓐ Ⓑ Ⓒ Ⓓ	25.	Ⓐ Ⓑ Ⓒ Ⓓ	32.	Ⓐ Ⓑ Ⓒ Ⓓ
5.	Ⓐ Ⓑ Ⓒ Ⓓ	12.	Ⓐ Ⓑ Ⓒ Ⓓ	19.	Ⓐ Ⓑ Ⓒ Ⓓ	26.	Ⓐ Ⓑ Ⓒ Ⓓ	33.	Ⓐ Ⓑ Ⓒ Ⓓ
6.	Ⓐ Ⓑ Ⓒ Ⓓ	13.	Ⓐ Ⓑ Ⓒ Ⓓ	20.	Ⓐ Ⓑ Ⓒ Ⓓ	27.	Ⓐ Ⓑ Ⓒ Ⓓ	34.	Ⓐ Ⓑ Ⓒ Ⓓ
7.	Ⓐ Ⓑ Ⓒ Ⓓ	14.	Ⓐ Ⓑ Ⓒ Ⓓ	21.	Ⓐ Ⓑ Ⓒ Ⓓ	28.	Ⓐ Ⓑ Ⓒ Ⓓ	35.	Ⓐ Ⓑ Ⓒ Ⓓ

ARTICLES AND PREPOSITIONS 

6

LEARNING OBJECTIVES

➤ Different Articles and their usage ➤ Different types of prepositions

PRACTICE EXERCISE

I. Choose the correct option and fill in the blanks.

1. Who is ___________ girl with Rajkumar.
   (A) the   (B) a
   (C) a / the   (D) none

2. We need a secretary with ______ good knowledge of English.
   (A) a   (B) the
   (C) a / the   (D) none

3. We're having __________ terrible weather.
   (A) a   (B) the
   (C) a / the   (D) none

4. What did you do with __________ stereo I lent you?
   (A) a   (B) the
   (C) a / the   (D) none

5. Could you close ___________ window?
   (A) a   (B) the
   (C) a / the   (D) none

6. My sister lives in ___________ London.
   (a) a   (B) the
   (C) a / the   (D) none

7. Emily is excited about being___________ grandmother
   (A) a   (B) the
   (C) a / the   (D) none

8. Life would be much less stressful without ___________ telephone.
   (A) a   (B) the
   (C) a / the   (D) none

9. ___________ Giant Panda is in danger of becoming extinct.
   (A) a   (B) the
   (C) a / the   (D) none

10. Mother is in __________ hospital. She has got kidney trouble.
    (A) a   (B) the
    (C) a / the   (D) none

11. I am studying ___________ life of Socrates.
    (A) a   (B) the
    (C) a / the   (D) none

12. He said that he wanted to become ___________ engineer.
    (A) a   (B) an
    (C) the   (D) none

13. He remained ___________ spinster all his life.
    (A) a   (B) the
    (C) a / the   (D) none

14. We have planted some roses in ___________ garden.
    (A) a   (B) the
    (C) a / the   (D) none

15. 'What is that noise?' 'I think it is ___________ airplane.'
    (A) a   (B) an
    (C) the   (D) none

II. Choose the correct answer from the options given. These are all prepositions of time.

16. I was on/in/at time for the inter-view.
17. She has just changed her job. She is now working at/on/in a bank.
18. The buses here are never in/on time. I always have to wait at least an hour.
19. The students had a party on/ in/ at Monday.
20. There is so much fog nowadays. If you take the train, you will not be able to reach in/at/time for the wedding.
21. You can get these fruits only at/on/in the summer.
22. She will call at/in/on time 6 am when she reaches London.
23. The Prime Minister is visiting Japan at/in/on March next year.
24. It is the premiere of the movie. Please be in/on/at time.
25. The shop opens at/on/in 10 am. We can get the things at that time.

HOTS (ACHIEVERS SECTION)

III. Fill in the blanks by putting a/an/the and complete the story:

The Ant and The Grasshopper

Once upon ___ time, there lived ___ ant and ___ grasshopper in ___ grassy meadow. It was during ___ hot summer season when ___ ant was toiling hard by collecting wheat grains from ___ farmer's field.On ___ other hand, ___ grasshopper spent all his time in singing and dancing. He would frequently call ___ ant to join him in singing and dancing.However, ___ ant would ignore him and continue with her work. ___ ant said that she was saving some food for ___ cold season and recommended ___ grasshopper to follow ___ same. ___ grasshopper didn't pay heed to her words and continued singing and dancing merrily. Soon summer faded to autumn and autumn to winter. Out of cold, ___ grasshopper lost his interest in singing and making merry. He was cold and hungry and had no place to take shelter from ___ snow outside. Suddenly he remembered about ___ ant and visited her for some food and shelter. ___ grasshopper made ___ approach to her for some food and shelter.She gently asked him to sing somewhere else and earn his food and shelter. It is then, ___ grasshopper realized that he should have saved up enough for ___ winter instead of wasting his time being lazy during summer in singing and dancing around.

IV. Underline the prepositions in this paragraph:

Gautam Buddha was born in 563 BC at Lumbini in Sakya Kshatriya clan of Kapilvastu on Vaiskha Purnima Day. His father Suddhodhana was the Saka ruler, his mother Mahamaya died after 7 days of his birth, so he was brought up by stepmother Gautami. He left home at the age of 29 years. He attained enlightenment at 35 years of age at Bodh Gaya under a pipal tree on the banks of Phalgu river on the 49th day of meditation.

1. Ⓐ Ⓑ Ⓒ Ⓓ	6. Ⓐ Ⓑ Ⓒ Ⓓ	11. Ⓐ Ⓑ Ⓒ Ⓓ	16 Ⓐ Ⓑ Ⓒ Ⓓ	21. Ⓐ Ⓑ Ⓒ Ⓓ
2. Ⓐ Ⓑ Ⓒ Ⓓ	7. Ⓐ Ⓑ Ⓒ Ⓓ	12. Ⓐ Ⓑ Ⓒ Ⓓ	17. Ⓐ Ⓑ Ⓒ Ⓓ	22. Ⓐ Ⓑ Ⓒ Ⓓ
3. Ⓐ Ⓑ Ⓒ Ⓓ	8. Ⓐ Ⓑ Ⓒ Ⓓ	13. Ⓐ Ⓑ Ⓒ Ⓓ	18. Ⓐ Ⓑ Ⓒ Ⓓ	23. Ⓐ Ⓑ Ⓒ Ⓓ
4. Ⓐ Ⓑ Ⓒ Ⓓ	9. Ⓐ Ⓑ Ⓒ Ⓓ	14. Ⓐ Ⓑ Ⓒ Ⓓ	19. Ⓐ Ⓑ Ⓒ Ⓓ	24. Ⓐ Ⓑ Ⓒ Ⓓ
5. Ⓐ Ⓑ Ⓒ Ⓓ	10. Ⓐ Ⓑ Ⓒ Ⓓ	15. Ⓐ Ⓑ Ⓒ Ⓓ	20. Ⓐ Ⓑ Ⓒ Ⓓ	25. Ⓐ Ⓑ Ⓒ Ⓓ

CONTRACTIONS AND CONJUNCTIONS

LEARNING OBJECTIVES

➤ Concept of Contraction
➤ Usage of Conjunctions

PRACTICE EXERCISE

I. Choose the correct contraction for the underlined words in each sentence.

1. <u>I am</u> going to the school.
   (A) I'am   (B) I'm
   (C) I'would   (D) None of these

2. <u>He is</u> driving his car.
   (A) He's   (B) He'is
   (C) He'll   (D) None of these

3. <u>She is</u> singing her favourite song.
   (A) She'is   (B) She'll
   (C) She's   (D) None of these

4. <u>It is</u> a huge cave.
   (A) It's   (B) Its
   (C) It'll   (D) 'It

5. <u>You are</u> very smart.
   (A) You's   (B) You'are
   (C) You're   (D) None of these

6. <u>We are</u> friends.
   (A) We're
   (B) We'are
   (C) We'll
   (D) None of these

7. <u>They are</u> going to climb that mountain.
   (A) They'are   (B) They're
   (C) They'r   (D) None of these

8. <u>I am</u> a student.
   (A) I'll
   (B) I'm
   (C) I' am
   (D) None of these

9. <u>That is</u> my house.
   (A) That'll   (B) That's
   (C) That'hv   (D) None of these

10. <u>Those are</u> rose bushes.
    (A) Those're   (B) Those'are
    (C) Those'hv   (D) None of these

11. <u>Who is</u> this?
    (A) Who'is   (B) Whois'
    (C) Who's   (D) None of these

12. <u>Where is</u> the book?
    (A) Where's   (B) Where'is
    (C) Where'll   (D) None of these

13. <u>Where are</u> we going tomorrow?
    (A) Where'is
    (B) Where're
    (C) Where'are
    (D) None of these

14. <u>I had</u> been to Chicago.
    (A) I'll   (B) I'had
    (C) I'd   (D) None of these

15. <u>You would</u> get that bed for the same price.
   (A) You'll
   (B) You'd
   (C) You'could
   (D) None of these

II. Choose the correct option to fill in the blanks in each sentence.

16. My sister loves animals. She just brought a puppy _______ a kitten home with her.
   (A) But   (B) Or
   (C) Yet   (D) And

17. I'd like to thank you _________ the lovely gift that you gave me.
   (A) Or   (B) For
   (C) And   (D) Yet

18. I want to go for a hike _________ I have to go to work today.
   (A) But   (B) Yet
   (C) Or   (D) For

19. They do not smoke, _________ do they play cards.
   (A) And   (B) Or
   (C) Nor   (D) Yet

20. I'm getting good grades _________ I study every day.
   (A) Or   (B) Yet
   (C) But   (D) Because

21. _________ the basement flooded, we spent all day cleaning up.
   (A) After
   (B) Although
   (C) Before
   (D) Even If

22. I don't want to go to the movies _________ I hate the smell of popcorn.
   (A) Although   (B) Because
   (C) Whenever   (D) So that

23. I paid Larry, _________ garden design work is top-notch.
   (A) Whenever   (B) Whose
   (C) After   (D) If

24. _________ spring arrives, we have to be prepared for more snow.
   (A) Because   (B) Until
   (C) Although   (D) Now that

25. _________ the alarm goes off, I hit the snooze button.
   (A) As soon as
   (B) Because
   (C) Before
   (D) Now that

26. She is neither polite _______ funny.
   (A) Or
   (B) Nor
   (C) Not
   (D) Yet

27. _______ that is the case, _________ I'm not surprised about what's happening.
   (A) If/then
   (B) No sooner/than
   (C) Scarcely/when
   (D) Whether/or

28. Have you made a decision about _______ to go to the movies _______ not?
   (A) If/then
   (B) Either/or
   (C) Whether/or
   (D) What with/and

29. _________ had I put my umbrella away, _________ it started raining.
   (A) No sooner/than
   (B) If/then
   (C) What with/and
   (D) Neither/nor

30. This salad is _______ delicious _______ healthy.
   (A) Whether/or
   (B) Both/and
   (C) Scarcely/when
   (D) Rather/than

Fill in the blanks with the appropriate contractions:

31. _________ have to finish your work today. It has to be submitted tomorrow.
    (A) You'd   (B) You'll
    (C) You've   (D) You're

32. If it hurts you so much I promise, I _________ do it again.
    (A) isn't   (B) won't
    (C) can't   (D) don't

33. We _________ neglect our duties towards our elders.
    (A) mustn't   (B) must'nt
    (C) needn't   (D) shan't

In each question, select the correct option that combine the two sentences without changing their meaning.

34. Do you want coffee now? Do you want it later?
    (A) Do you want coffee now and later?
    (B) Do you want coffee now but not later?
    (C) Do you want coffee now or later?
    (D) Do you want now but also coffee later?

35. Roja did not meet Shalini. She did not meet Malini.
    (A) Roja either did not meet Shalini or Malini.
    (B) Roja neither met Shalini or Malini.
    (C) Roja neither met Shalini and Malini.
    (D) Roja met neither Shalini nor Malini.

—Darken Your Choice with HB Pencil—

1.	Ⓐ Ⓑ Ⓒ Ⓓ	8.	Ⓐ Ⓑ Ⓒ Ⓓ	15.	Ⓐ Ⓑ Ⓒ Ⓓ	22	Ⓐ Ⓑ Ⓒ Ⓓ	29.	Ⓐ Ⓑ Ⓒ Ⓓ
2.	Ⓐ Ⓑ Ⓒ Ⓓ	9.	Ⓐ Ⓑ Ⓒ Ⓓ	16.	Ⓐ Ⓑ Ⓒ Ⓓ	23.	Ⓐ Ⓑ Ⓒ Ⓓ	30.	Ⓐ Ⓑ Ⓒ Ⓓ
3.	Ⓐ Ⓑ Ⓒ Ⓓ	10.	Ⓐ Ⓑ Ⓒ Ⓓ	17.	Ⓐ Ⓑ Ⓒ Ⓓ	24.	Ⓐ Ⓑ Ⓒ Ⓓ	31.	Ⓐ Ⓑ Ⓒ Ⓓ
4.	Ⓐ Ⓑ Ⓒ Ⓓ	11.	Ⓐ Ⓑ Ⓒ Ⓓ	18.	Ⓐ Ⓑ Ⓒ Ⓓ	25.	Ⓐ Ⓑ Ⓒ Ⓓ	32.	Ⓐ Ⓑ Ⓒ Ⓓ
5.	Ⓐ Ⓑ Ⓒ Ⓓ	12.	Ⓐ Ⓑ Ⓒ Ⓓ	19.	Ⓐ Ⓑ Ⓒ Ⓓ	26.	Ⓐ Ⓑ Ⓒ Ⓓ	33.	Ⓐ Ⓑ Ⓒ Ⓓ
6.	Ⓐ Ⓑ Ⓒ Ⓓ	13.	Ⓐ Ⓑ Ⓒ Ⓓ	20.	Ⓐ Ⓑ Ⓒ Ⓓ	27.	Ⓐ Ⓑ Ⓒ Ⓓ	34.	Ⓐ Ⓑ Ⓒ Ⓓ
7.	Ⓐ Ⓑ Ⓒ Ⓓ	14.	Ⓐ Ⓑ Ⓒ Ⓓ	21.	Ⓐ Ⓑ Ⓒ Ⓓ	28.	Ⓐ Ⓑ Ⓒ Ⓓ	35.	Ⓐ Ⓑ Ⓒ Ⓓ

TENSES

LEARNING OBJECTIVES

➤ Usage of tenses in English

PRACTICE EXERCISE

I. Choose the correct option to complete the following sentences.

1. The university opens/opened on the 17th July every year.
2. Kusum called/will call me as soon as he comes.
3. The water is already boiled it will spill over/spills over if you don't turn off the heat.
4. I talks/talked to him yesterday.
5. Fish swim/will swim in water.
6. The next train is/was at 6:15 am tomorrow morning.
7. Shakespeare said/says, what's in a name?
8. It will take us/takes us twenty more minutes to reach there, have patience.
9. Please be quiet, the chief guest is going to speak/speak in a moment.
10. I heated/will heat the food for her yesterday.
11. I will see if the letter comes/came today.
12. The sails/ship sailed out of the harbour in time last week.
13. Sania will get/gets the medal for us in the coming Olympics.
14. I have decided that I went/am going to go to Ladakh this summer.
15. My alarm ring/rings at 5:30 every morning.

II. Complete the following sentences with the correct form of the verb.

16. I ____________ milk every night. (present continuous – habit)
    (A) Drink
    (B) Drank
    (C) Will drink
    (D) Drinks

17. The Bhagavat Gita says, your duty is to ____________ your work as best as you can. (Present – quote)
    (A) Will finish
    (B) Finished
    (C) Finish
    (D) Finishes

18. It is ____________ cats and dogs, the clouds are all black. (future – prediction)
    (A) Rains
    (B) Rained
    (C) Going to rain
    (D) Rain

19. The parade _______________ at 6 am every year on 26th January. I watch it. (present – habit)
(A) Will begin
(B) Began
(C) Begin
(D) Begins

20. I just spoke to her. She __________ upset. (past)
(A) Seem
(B) Seemed
(C) Will seem
(D) Is going to seem

21. Every mother _____________ her child. (present – statement)
(A) Loves
(B) Loved
(C) Love
(D) Will love

22. We have just started from Shimla. We ___________ Delhi after ten hours. (future)
(A) Reached
(B) Will reach
(C) Reach
(D) Reaches

23. I always ________________ an umbrella here. (present – habit)
(A) Will carry
(B) Carried
(C) Carry
(D) Carrying

24. Let's quickly go inside. It's _______ any minute now.
(A) Going to rain
(B) Rained
(C) Rain
(D) Rains

25. I think she ________________ a song, she is a good singer. (future – prediction)
(A) Sings
(B) Will sing
(C) Sang
(D) Sing

26. Here _______________ the cake! (present – statement)
(A) Was
(B) Will be
(C) Is going to be
(D) Is

27. If she __________, we will go to the museum. (present – clause of time and condition)
(A) Came
(B) Will come
(C) Come
(D) Comes

28. Renu __________ maths. (present – habit)
(A) Like
(B) Liked
(C) Likes
(D) Will like

29. We _____________ the new car last month. (simple past)
(A) Booked
(B) Will book
(C) Books
(D) Book

30. Sita ________________ at ram and falls in love with him. (present – dramatic)
(A) Looked
(B) Looks
(C) Will look
(D) Look

Read the passage given below and complete the sentences using the verb given in the brackets:

Water in the sea and on the ground constantly __ (31) __ (evaporate) due to heat of the sun. Water__ (32) __ (get) converted into vapour which __ (33) __ (go) upwards in the atmosphere. Water vapours then __ (34) __ (condense) on the dust particles to form clouds.

When clouds __ (35) __ (go) up, they condense into water which __ (36) __ (come) down again as rains. __ (37) __ (you know) what __ (38) __ (happen) to this water? All of it __ (39) __ (not seep) into earth. Most of it __ (40) __ (collect) in the sea and other reservoirs of water on land. It evaporates again, __ (41) __ (rise) in the sky and __ (42) __ (convert) into rainwater.

1. Ⓐ Ⓑ Ⓒ Ⓓ	7. Ⓐ Ⓑ Ⓒ Ⓓ	13. Ⓐ Ⓑ Ⓒ Ⓓ	19 Ⓐ Ⓑ Ⓒ Ⓓ	25. Ⓐ Ⓑ Ⓒ Ⓓ
2. Ⓐ Ⓑ Ⓒ Ⓓ	8. Ⓐ Ⓑ Ⓒ Ⓓ	14. Ⓐ Ⓑ Ⓒ Ⓓ	20. Ⓐ Ⓑ Ⓒ Ⓓ	26. Ⓐ Ⓑ Ⓒ Ⓓ
3. Ⓐ Ⓑ Ⓒ Ⓓ	9. Ⓐ Ⓑ Ⓒ Ⓓ	15. Ⓐ Ⓑ Ⓒ Ⓓ	21. Ⓐ Ⓑ Ⓒ Ⓓ	27. Ⓐ Ⓑ Ⓒ Ⓓ
4. Ⓐ Ⓑ Ⓒ Ⓓ	10. Ⓐ Ⓑ Ⓒ Ⓓ	16. Ⓐ Ⓑ Ⓒ Ⓓ	22. Ⓐ Ⓑ Ⓒ Ⓓ	28. Ⓐ Ⓑ Ⓒ Ⓓ
5. Ⓐ Ⓑ Ⓒ Ⓓ	11. Ⓐ Ⓑ Ⓒ Ⓓ	17. Ⓐ Ⓑ Ⓒ Ⓓ	23. Ⓐ Ⓑ Ⓒ Ⓓ	29. Ⓐ Ⓑ Ⓒ Ⓓ
6. Ⓐ Ⓑ Ⓒ Ⓓ	12. Ⓐ Ⓑ Ⓒ Ⓓ	18. Ⓐ Ⓑ Ⓒ Ⓓ	24. Ⓐ Ⓑ Ⓒ Ⓓ	30. Ⓐ Ⓑ Ⓒ Ⓓ

JUMBLE WORDS AND IDIOMS/PROVERBS

LEARNING OBJECTIVES

➤ Jumbled words
➤ Idioms
➤ Proverbs

PRACTICE EXERCISE

1. Direction: Choose the correct option. A man of straw
   (A) A man of no substance
   (B) A very active person
   (C) A worthy fellow
   (D) An unreasonable person

2. Direction: Choose the correct option. A black sheep
   (A) An unlucky person
   (B) A lucky person
   (C) An odd member of a group
   (D) A partner who takes no share of the profits

3. Direction: Choose the correct option. To be the question
   (A) To refer to
   (B) To take for granted
   (C) To raise objections
   (D) To be discussed

4. Direction: Choose the correct option. To play second fiddle
   (A) To be happy, cheerful and healthy
   (B) To reduce importance of one's senior
   (C) To support the role and view of another person
   (D) To do back seat driving

5. Direction: Choose the correct option. To leave someone in the lurch
   (A) To compromise with someone
   (B) To annoy someone
   (C) To put someone at ease
   (D) To desert someone in his difficulties

6. Direction: Choose the correct option. To pick holes
   (A) To find some reason to quarrel
   (B) To destroy something
   (C) To criticise someone
   (D) To cut some part of an item

7. Direction: Choose the correct option. To put one's hand to plough
   (A) To take up agricultural farming
   (B) To take a difficult task
   (C) To get into unnecessary things
   (D) Take interest in technical work

8. Direction: Choose the correct option. To be above board
   (A) To have a good height
   (B) To be honest in any business deal
   (C) They have no debts
   (D) To try to be beautiful

9. Direction: Choose the correct option. To end in smoke
   (A) To make completely understand
   (B) To ruin oneself
   (C) To excite great applause
   (D) To overcome someone

10. Direction: Choose the correct option. To chave an axe to grind
    (A) A private end to serve
    (B) To fail to arouse interest
    (C) To have no result
    (D) To work for both sides

11. Direction: Choose the correct option. To cry wolf
    (A) To listen eagerly
    (B) To give false alarm
    (C) To turn pale
    (D) To keep off starvation

12. Direction: Choose the correct option. To drive home
    (A) To find ones roots
    (B) To return to place of rest
    (C) Back to original position
    (D) To emphasise

13. Direction: Choose the correct option. To catch a tartar
    (A) To trap wanted criminal with great difficulty
    (B) To catch a dangerous person
    (C) To meet with disaster
    (D) To deal with a person who is more than ones match

14. Direction: Choose the correct option. To keeps one's temper
    (A) To become hungry
    (B) To preserve ones energy
    (C) To be in good mood
    (D) To be aloof from

15. Direction: Choose the correct option. To make clean breast of
    (A) To gain prominence
    (B) To praise oneself
    (C) To confess without of reserve
    (D) To destroy before it blooms

16. Direction: Choose the correct option. To smell a rat
    (A) To see signs of plague epidemic
    (B) To get bad small of a bad dead rat
    (C) To suspect foul dealings
    (D) To be in a bad mood

17. Direction: Choose the correct option. To hit the nail right on the head
    (A) To do the right thing
    (B) To destroy ones reputation
    (C) To announce ones fixed views
    (D) To teach someone a lesson

18. Direction: Choose the correct option. To set one's face against
    (A) To oppose with determination
    (B) To judge by appearance
    (C) To get out of difficulty
    (D) To look at one steadily

19. Direction: Choose the correct option. To bait a trap
    (A) To plan an idea
    (B) To make conspiracy
    (C) To get into problem
    (D) To spread a trap-cage

20. Direction: Choose the correct option. Cold shoulder
    (A) discourtesy
    (B) discomfort
    (C) disrespect
    (D) discipline

21. Direction: In list I the idioms are given and in list II the sentence is completed in a way that the meaning of the idiom becomes clearer. Match the following:

	List I		List II
A.	You should keep him at arm's length	1.	he obviously has much better skills.
B.	He is sitting on the fence, trying to	2.	so do not worry.
C.	He is willing to play second fiddle although	3.	see which side he should cheer for.
D.	I have the whole plan at my fingertips	4.	because he may have a bad influence on you.

(A) A-1   B-2   C-3   D-4
(B) A-2   B-3   C-4   D-1
(C) A-3   B-4   C-1   D-2
(D) A-4   B-3   C-1   D-2

22. Direction: In list I the idioms are given and in list II the sentence is completed in a way that the meaning of the idiom becomes clearer. Match the following:

	List I		List II
A.	A bird in the hand is worth two in the bush so	1.	it will grow out of control.
B.	I paid through the nose for	2.	get the job at first.
C.	Janet broke the ice and started	3.	the over-priced video game.
D.	We have to nip the problem in the bud or	4.	a conversation with the shy boy.

23. Direction: In list I the idioms are given and in list II the sentence is completed in a way that the meaning of the idiom becomes clearer. Match the following:

	List I		List II
A.	He held his tongue and managed	1.	he is the one who did it.
B.	She is a greenhorn and it takes time for her	2.	so you may like it but he may not.
C.	I am cock sure that	3.	to keep the secret to himself.
D.	One man's meat is another man's poison	4.	to learn all the skills needed for the job.

(A) A-1   B-2   C-3   D-4
(B) A-2   B-3   C-4   D-1
(C) A-3   B-4   C-1   D-2
(D) A-4   B-3   C-1   D-2

24. Direction: In list I the idioms are given and in list II the sentence is completed in a way that the meaning of the idiom becomes clearer. Match the following:

	List I		List II
A.	By hook or by crook, we have to submit	1.	the assignment by the end of this month.
B.	You must not put all your eggs in one basket	2.	try to find some alternatives.

| C. | His words carry weight | 3. | because he is well respected. |
| D. | Half a loaf is better than none | 4. | be grateful for what you get. |

(A) A-1   B-2   C-3   D-4
(B) A-2   B-3   C-4   D-1
(C) A-3   B-4   C-1   D-2
(D) A-4   B-3   C-1   D-2

25. Direction: In list I the idioms are given and in list II the sentence is completed in a way that the meaning of the idiom becomes clearer. Match the following:

	List I		List II
A.	He took the law into his	1.	to impress his boss.
B.	He was like a dog with two tails	2.	my grandfather firmly believes in the saying.
C.	Colin put his best foot forward in the project	3.	own hands and killed the robber.
D.	"Spare the rod and spoil the child"	4.	when he won the final game.

(A) A-1   B-2   C-3   D-4
(B) A-2   B-3   C-4   D-1
(C) A-3   B-4   C-1   D-2
(D) A-4   B-3   C-1   D-2

1.	Ⓐ Ⓑ Ⓒ Ⓓ	6.	Ⓐ Ⓑ Ⓒ Ⓓ	11.	Ⓐ Ⓑ Ⓒ Ⓓ	16	Ⓐ Ⓑ Ⓒ Ⓓ	21.	Ⓐ Ⓑ Ⓒ Ⓓ
2.	Ⓐ Ⓑ Ⓒ Ⓓ	7.	Ⓐ Ⓑ Ⓒ Ⓓ	12.	Ⓐ Ⓑ Ⓒ Ⓓ	17.	Ⓐ Ⓑ Ⓒ Ⓓ	22.	Ⓐ Ⓑ Ⓒ Ⓓ
3.	Ⓐ Ⓑ Ⓒ Ⓓ	8.	Ⓐ Ⓑ Ⓒ Ⓓ	13.	Ⓐ Ⓑ Ⓒ Ⓓ	18.	Ⓐ Ⓑ Ⓒ Ⓓ	23.	Ⓐ Ⓑ Ⓒ Ⓓ
4.	Ⓐ Ⓑ Ⓒ Ⓓ	9.	Ⓐ Ⓑ Ⓒ Ⓓ	14.	Ⓐ Ⓑ Ⓒ Ⓓ	19.	Ⓐ Ⓑ Ⓒ Ⓓ	24.	Ⓐ Ⓑ Ⓒ Ⓓ
5.	Ⓐ Ⓑ Ⓒ Ⓓ	10.	Ⓐ Ⓑ Ⓒ Ⓓ	15.	Ⓐ Ⓑ Ⓒ Ⓓ	20.	Ⓐ Ⓑ Ⓒ Ⓓ	25.	Ⓐ Ⓑ Ⓒ Ⓓ

COMPREHENSION

PRACTICE EXERCISE

Comprehension 1

Read the following story and answer the questions which follow.

There was once an ant. His name was Anand. He was always joyful, energetic and hardworking. As a result, he was fit as a fiddle. Anand used to work at the sugar factory because he liked eating sweets a lot. He always wanted to be near sweets. He used to reach office on time, finish his work on time and happily come back home in time to see his favourite TV shows. He was happy as a clam in mud at high tide.

Anand had a friend, Gautam. Gautam was a grasshopper and even though they were friends, they were both as different as chalk and cheese. He hardly ever worked and spent most of his evenings at Anand's place for dinner. He was also very jealous of Anand as he thought that Anand had an easy job. He always said that if he had such an easy job, he would have made a lot of money too. That is the reason why the grasshopper kept on becoming green with envy.

Summers were alright but winters were very tough on the Gautam. Even Anand could only save so much grain for the winter months. If he would have shared all his grains with Gautam then both of them would have died of hunger.

Once when Anand had refused to give Gautam any food, Gautam decided to go to the king of the jungle, the lion. Gautam said to the lion, "Is this not unfair? I am starving here and Anand is sitting comfortably at home with a hot supper? There should be a law which ensure that every body gets food when hungry."

The lion smiled and said, "You reap what you sow, since you didn't work all year, you are hungry. Since Anand has worked so hard, he has all the comforts! This is justice! I can't take the fruits of his labour away from him. He has earned his reward." Gautam had to go home without any free food but with an important lesson.

1. You have read the following idioms in the passage, based on your understanding, write down their meanings:

   (A) Happy as a clam in the mud in high tide.

   ____

   ____

   ____

   (B) As different as chalk and cheese.

   ____

   ____

   ____

   (C) Become green with envy.

   ____

   ____

   ____

   (D) Reap what you sow.

   ____

   ____

   ____

OLYMPIAD WORKBOOK (IEO) CLASS– 4

(E) Fit as a fiddle.

____

____

____

2. Answer the following questions on the basis of the story you have read above.

(A) Where did Anand work?

____

____

____

(B) Did he like working there?

____

____

____

(C) Was the Gautam like Ananda?

____

____

____

(D) Where did Gautam take most of his dinners?

____

____

____

(E) How did Anand prepare for the winters?

____

____

____

(f) Who did Gautam go to with his complaint?

____

____

____

(g) What did Gautam tell the king?

____

____

____

(h) Did the king agree with Gautam?

____

____

____

(i) What did the king tell Gautam?

____

____

____

(j) What did you learn from this story?

____

____

____

Comprehension 2

Read the following dialogue and answer the questions which follow.

Gopal: Did you know that it was Revathy's birthday yesterday?

Anish: No, I was busy with my cricket practice all morning.

G: That's right, you guys are preparing for the zonal finals. How is the practice coming along?

A: We're doing well. I think we have a good chance.

G: Great! I hope you guys win the zonal match this year! We havn't won in the last three years.

A: We are working very hard. We should be able to get the cup this year. Did you go to Revathy's party?

G: Yes, I did. It was a great party. We all went paintball shooting in the afternoon and then for lunch at McDonald's.

A: That sounds great! I have never been paintball shooting. Did you guys go to the outlet near Sec-18?

G: Yes. Her parents had rented the whole place for two hours and we played in two teams. Revathy was the captain for one of the teams and Aisha was the captain for the other.

A: That sounds great. Who won?

G: Revathy won. We all were happy that she won during her birthday celebrations. After wards, we went to McDonald's and she cut a cake there. We were also gifted with little toys which come with happy meal.

A: It sounds like I missed out on a lot of things. Was Rohan there? He left the practice early saying that he had to go to a party. I think he must have met you guys.

G: Yes. He joined us only at McDonalds. He came with us to Revathy's house and he even won the first round of games that we played on her play station.

A: What else did you guys do?

G: There was a very nice clown as well. He played a lot of tricks and made us laugh a lot. There was a magician who showed us a lot of magic tricks. He made a rabbit disappear and showed us a handkerchief which was about a mile long!

A: I saw a trick like that once in a magic show I saw with my dad in Mumbai once. We also saw a lot of gymnasts who swayed so high on the trapeze that it looked like they were hanging from the sky.

G: I would love to see that! I will ask my dad to take me to Mumbai to see that show.

A: I think they have that show in Delhi as well. I saw a similar thing in youtube some days ago. My brother showed it to me.

G: Let's see it now? I also want to see the highlights of the football match from last night. Have you finished your homework?

A: I finished it two hours ago. I am completely free. Even my mother gave me permission to use the internet for an hour.

3. Whose birthday was it yesterday?

____

____

4. Why didn't Anish go to Revathy's birthday party?

____

____

____

5. Does the cricket team have a good chance in the Zonal finals?

____

____

____

6. How long has the cricket team not won?

____

____

____

7. Did Gopal go to Revathy's party?

____

____

____

8. Where did the kids go in the afternoon?

____

____

____

9. Where did the kids go for lunch?

____

____

____

10. Has Anish ever been paintballing?

____

____

____

11. Which paintball outlet did the guys go to?

____

12. How long had Revathy's parents rented the paintball outlet?

13. Who were the captains for the two paintball teams?

14. Who won the paintball competition?

15. What kind of toys did the kids get at McDonald's?

16. Was Rohan at Revathy's birthday party?

17. Where did he join the party?

18. Who won the first round of games on the play station?

19. Who made the kids laugh a lot at Revathy's birthday party?

20. What tricks did the magicians show?

21. Who looked like they were hanging from the sky?

22. What do Anish and Gopal decide to do online?

1.	Ⓐ Ⓑ Ⓒ Ⓓ	6.	Ⓐ Ⓑ Ⓒ Ⓓ	11.	Ⓐ Ⓑ Ⓒ Ⓓ	16	Ⓐ Ⓑ Ⓒ Ⓓ	21.	Ⓐ Ⓑ Ⓒ Ⓓ
2.	Ⓐ Ⓑ Ⓒ Ⓓ	7.	Ⓐ Ⓑ Ⓒ Ⓓ	12.	Ⓐ Ⓑ Ⓒ Ⓓ	17.	Ⓐ Ⓑ Ⓒ Ⓓ	22.	Ⓐ Ⓑ Ⓒ Ⓓ
3.	Ⓐ Ⓑ Ⓒ Ⓓ	8.	Ⓐ Ⓑ Ⓒ Ⓓ	13.	Ⓐ Ⓑ Ⓒ Ⓓ	18.	Ⓐ Ⓑ Ⓒ Ⓓ		
4.	Ⓐ Ⓑ Ⓒ Ⓓ	9.	Ⓐ Ⓑ Ⓒ Ⓓ	14.	Ⓐ Ⓑ Ⓒ Ⓓ	19.	Ⓐ Ⓑ Ⓒ Ⓓ		
5.	Ⓐ Ⓑ Ⓒ Ⓓ	10.	Ⓐ Ⓑ Ⓒ Ⓓ	15.	Ⓐ Ⓑ Ⓒ Ⓓ	20.	Ⓐ Ⓑ Ⓒ Ⓓ		

SPOKEN AND WRITTEN EXPRESSION; PUNCTUATION

PRACTICE EXERCISE

I. Which occasion do the following belong to?

1. Hi, this is Ranjan –
2. I would love to –
3. I am sorry for –
4. Good evening –
5. It's okay –
6. Can I introduce Ria –
7. Forget about it –
8. Sorry, I would not be able to –
9. No harm done –
10. It's good to see you –
11. Hi Parul, how are you? –
12. Sure, no problem –
13. Please forgive me for –
14. Good afternoon –
15. Don't mention it –

II. Choose the best response from the options given below:

16. Why did you run away?
    (A) I was frightened by the sound of thunder.
    (B) Were you tired?
    (C) Were you happy?
    (D) None of the above.

17. I would like to finish my assignment today.
    (A) Would you be able to?
    (B) Won't you be able?
    (C) Will you be able to?
    (D) None of the above.

18. Rakshak is so boring, I don't want to invite him.
    (A) I must invite him.
    (B) I understand your problem, but you will have to.
    (C) You will invite him.
    (d) Both (b) and (c)

19. Where is the boss going during vacation?
    (A) I don't have any idea.
    (B) I really wonder where he is going?
    (C) Don't you think where he is going!
    (D) All of the above.

20. Could I borrow some storage devices from you?
    (A) Why do you need them for?
    (B) What do you need them for?
    (C) What do you need them?
    (D) Both (b) and (c)

21. Haven't you put on weight recently?
    (A) No, there isn't.
    (B) Yes, I did
    (C) Yes, I have.
    (D) Both (A) and (B)

22. Ali: "My friend doesn't work very hard"
    Riya: "_________?"
    Ali: "Of course I do!"
    (A) Do you?
    (B) Don't you?
    (C) Have you?
    (D) All of these.

OLYMPIAD WORKBOOK (IEO) CLASS– 4

23. Ann: "Where's Rajghat?"
Jim: "_______________."
Ann: "Can you tell me where Rajghat is?"
(A) Repeat
(B) I can't understand.
(C) I beg your pardon.
(D) I could not understand.
24. How much are these mangoes?
(A) One kilo for twenty five rupees.
(B) Twenty five rupees a kilo.
(C) One kilo in twenty five rupees.
(D) One kilo on twenty five rupees.
25. Are you sure you will win?
(A) I am afraid I will.
(B) I think I will
(C) I'm sure I will.
(D) All of these.

——— Darken Your Choice with HB Pencil ———

1.	(A) (B) (C) (D)	6.	(A) (B) (C) (D)	11.	(A) (B) (C) (D)	16	(A) (B) (C) (D)	21.	(A) (B) (C) (D)
2.	(A) (B) (C) (D)	7.	(A) (B) (C) (D)	12.	(A) (B) (C) (D)	17.	(A) (B) (C) (D)	22.	(A) (B) (C) (D)
3.	(A) (B) (C) (D)	8.	(A) (B) (C) (D)	13.	(A) (B) (C) (D)	18.	(A) (B) (C) (D)	23.	(A) (B) (C) (D)
4.	(A) (B) (C) (D)	9.	(A) (B) (C) (D)	14.	(A) (B) (C) (D)	19.	(A) (B) (C) (D)	24.	(A) (B) (C) (D)
5.	(A) (B) (C) (D)	10.	(A) (B) (C) (D)	15.	(A) (B) (C) (D)	20.	(A) (B) (C) (D)	25.	(A) (B) (C) (D)

MODEL TEST PAPER

MULTIPLE CHOICE QUESTIONS

SECTION I: Word And Structure Knowledge

Direction (1–5): Choose the correct antonyms

1. Polite
   (A) Rude
   (B) Happy
   (C) Manners
   (D) Avoid
2. Permanent
   (A) Same
   (B) Always
   (C) Transient
   (D) Temporary
3. Virtue
   (A) Evil
   (B) Bad
   (C) Vice
   (D) Less
4. Straight
   (A) Circle
   (B) Crooked
   (C) Line
   (D) Narrow
5. Success
   (A) Lose
   (B) Failure
   (C) Immense
   (D) Fail

Direction (6–10): Choose the correct synonyms.

6. Eatable
   (A) Edible
   (B) Oral
   (C) Tasty
   (D) Poisonous
7. Indolent
   (A) Calm
   (B) Industrious
   (C) Furious
   (D) Lazy
8. Feeble
   (A) Unable
   (B) Alert
   (C) Weak
   (D) Secure
9. Scarce
   (A) Usual
   (B) Rare
   (C) Plenty
   (D) Unavailable
10. Real
    (A) Genuine
    (B) Ready
    (C) Lean
    (D) Fake

Direction (11–15): Fill in the blanks with correct prepositions.

11. A lamp was hung ______ my head.
    (A) At
    (B) Over
    (C) Above
    (D) On
12. He sailed ______ the sea.
    (A) Across
    (B) Through
    (C) On
    (D) To
13. He returned ______ many days.
    (A) For
    (B) After
    (C) From
    (D) Into
14. He is not ______ home just now.
    (A) At
    (B) On
    (C) To
    (D) For
15. I will tell him ____ call you.
    (A) On
    (B) For
    (C) At
    (D) To

Directions (16–20): Make a meaningful word.

16. Glaryoss
    (A) Ossalgry
    (B) lossgary
    (C) sarsyolg
    (D) Glossary
17. Micag
    (A) Lmcag
    (B) Magic
    (C) Cagmi
    (D) Migac
18. Copomse
    (A) Compose
    (B) Seomcop
    (C) Ompocse
    (D) Seocmop
19. Flerify
    (A) Elfrify
    (B) Fleriyf
    (C) Firefly
    (D) Flyfire
20. Matecil
    (A) Cetamli
    (B) Climate
    (C) limatec
    (D) Mliatec

Pollution is the degradation of natural environment by the introduction of external substances directly or indirectly into natural resources such as air and water. Human health, ecosystem and aquatic and terrestrial biodiversity may be affected and altered permanently due to pollution. Pollution occurs when ecosystems cannot get rid of substances introduced into the environment. The critical threshold of its ability to naturally eliminate substances is compromised and the balance of the ecosystem is broken.

The sources and reasons of pollution are numerous. The identification of these different pollutants and their effects on ecosystems is complex. They can come from natural disasters or the result of human activity such as oil spills, chemical spills, nuclear accidents etc. These can have terrible consequences on people and the planet: destruction of the biodiversity, increased mortality of the human and animal species, destruction of natural habitat, damage caused to the quality of soil, water and air.

Preventing pollution and protecting the environment necessitate the application of the principles of sustainable development. We have to consider the needs of today without compromising the ability of future generations to meet their needs. This means that we should remedy existing pollution, but also anticipate and prevent future pollution sources in order to protect the environment and public health. Any environmental damage must be punishable by law, and polluters should pay compensation for the damage caused to the environment.

Answer the following questions based on passage given.

21. The degradation of natural environment by external substances introduced directly or indirectly is known as
    (A) Pollution   (B) Disastrous
    (C) Harmful   (D) Polluters

22. Pollution only has a temporary effect
    (A) True   (B) False

23. Only the aquatic and terrestrial ecosystems are disturbed.
    (A) True   (B) False

24. The ecosystem can always cope with pollutants.
    (A) False   (B) True

25. Pollution is caused by
    (A) Aliens
    (B) Natural disasters
    (C) Both A and D
    (D) Human activity

Mickey Mouse is a cartoon character who has become an icon for the Walt Disney Company. Mickey Mouse is short for Mitchell Mouse. It was created in 1928 by **Walt Disney** and **Ub Iwerks** and voiced by **Walt Disney**. The first appearance of Mickey Mouse was in *Plane Crazy* on May 15, 1928. But the Walt Disney Company celebrates Mickey Mouse birthday on November 18, 1928 upon the release of *Steamboat Willie*, because it is the first Mickey Mouse Cartoon with sound. The anthropomorphic mouse has developed along the years. He first appeared in colour in 1935. The first **Technicolor Disney** film was **Flowers and Trees** in 1932. He also evolved from being simply a character in animated cartoons and comic strips to become one of the most recognizable symbols in the world. Popularity has grown around the world. This was due to his angelic nature. Mickey never does anything immoral. However, in 2009 the Walt Disney Company announced that they will begin to re-brand the Mickey Mouse character by moving away from his pleasant, cheerful image and reintroducing the more devious side of his personality, starting with the upcoming **Epic Mickey,** a Mickey Mouse video game. The Walt Disney Company thus intends to show the mischievous side of Mickey's personality.

Answer the following questions based on passage given.

26. When is Mickey Mouse's birthday?
   (A) May 18, 1932
   (B) November 18, 1928
   (C) November 15, 1935
   (D) May 15, 1928

27. The first Mickey Mouse with sound appeared in 'Steamboat Willie'.
   (A) True   (B) False

28. The first Technicolour film was 'Steamboat Willie'.
   (A) False   (B) True

29. Animated means
   (A) Funny jokes
   (B) Full of life
   (C) Made using animation techniques
   (D) Animal related

30. What is 'Epic Mickey'?
   (A) Comic book   (B) Movie
   (C) Comic strip   (D) A video game

SECTION III: Spoken and Written Expression

Choose the correct option.

31. Malini: Would you please call your mother?
   Chinki:
   (A) Yes, just wait a minute.
   (B) Maybe, if you give me a chocolate.
   (C) I don't feel like it.
   (D) No.

32. Tony: We never see you these days.
   Mack:
   (A) I forgot about you all.
   (B) I had some work.
   (C) Sorry, I have been out of town.
   (D) Why are you bothering me?

33. Boss: Try to get the deal signed by today.
   Secretary:
   (A) You should do it since you're the Boss.
   (B) You do it.
   (C) I'll do my best.
   (D) I can't.

34. Reggie: I got the highest marks in class!
   Betty:
   (A) I wanted to get the highest.
   (B) Congratulations!
   (C) You didn't deserve them.
   (D) Who cares?

35. Uncle: How are you?
   Rima:
   (A) Do you really care?
   (B) You don't need to know.
   (C) Fine.
   (D) Good, how are you?

Darken Your Choice with HB Pencil

1.	A B C D	8.	A B C D	15.	A B C D	22.	A B C D	29.	A B C D
2.	A B C D	9.	A B C D	16.	A B C D	23.	A B C D	30.	A B C D
3.	A B C D	10.	A B C D	17.	A B C D	24.	A B C D	31.	A B C D
4.	A B C D	11.	A B C D	18.	A B C D	25.	A B C D	32.	A B C D
5.	A B C D	12.	A B C D	19.	A B C D	26.	A B C D	33.	A B C D
6.	A B C D	13.	A B C D	20.	A B C D	27.	A B C D	34.	A B C D
7.	A B C D	14.	A B C D	21.	A B C D	28.	A B C D	35.	A B C D

1. VOCABULARY

Answer Key

I

1. Priest	2. Queen	3. Boxes	4. Misinformed	5. Driving
6. Almost	7. Thief	8. Supplied	9. Played	10. Unaware

II

11. Stationery	12. Cutlery	13. Spices	14. Clothes	15. Toiletries
16. Utensils	17. Spices	18. Stationery	19. Clothes	20. Spices

III

21. Love	22. Anger	23. Fear	24. Love	25. Shame
26. Anger	27. Sadness	28. Surprise	29. Fear	30. Love
31. Anger	32. Sadness	33. Surprise	34. Shame	35. Fear

HOTS (ACHIEVERS SECTION)

36. Do you like Marathi food?
37. What is your roll number?
38. Dogs, sheep, horses, cows, chicken
39. Sqrirrels, cows, dogs, pigeons, goats
40. Sadness

2. A WORLD OF WORDS

Answer Key

I

1. (A)	2. (A)	3. (D)	4. (C)	5. (D)	6. (D)	7. (B)	8. (A)	9. (D)	10. (D)
11. (B)	12. (A)	13. (C)	14. (A)	15. (C)	16. (C)	17. (A)	18. (A)	19. (B)	20. (A)

<table>
<tr><td colspan="10" align="center">II</td></tr>
<tr><td>21. (A)</td><td>22. (A)</td><td>23. (D)</td><td>24. (D)</td><td>25. (A)</td><td>26. (A)</td><td>27. (D)</td><td>28. (B)</td><td>29. (D)</td><td>30. (D)</td></tr>
</table>

HOTS (ACHIEVERS SECTION)

31. (C)	32. (A)	33. (A)	34. (B)	35. (A)

3. NOUNS AND PRONOUNS

Answer Key

<table>
<tr><td colspan="10" align="center">I</td></tr>
<tr><td>1. (A)</td><td>2. (C)</td><td>3. (D)</td><td>4. (B)</td><td>5. (C)</td><td>6. (D)</td><td>7. (C)</td><td>8. (C)</td><td>9. (D)</td><td>10. (A)</td></tr>
<tr><td>11. (A)</td><td>12. (C)</td><td>13. (B)</td><td>14. (B)</td><td>15. (A)</td><td></td><td></td><td></td><td></td><td></td></tr>
<tr><td colspan="10" align="center">II</td></tr>
<tr><td>16. (D)</td><td>17. (C)</td><td>18. (B)</td><td>19. (D)</td><td>20. (A)</td><td>21. (D)</td><td>22. (A)</td><td>23. (B)</td><td>24. (D)</td><td>25. (A)</td></tr>
<tr><td>26. (B)</td><td>27. (C)</td><td>28. (B)</td><td>29. (C)</td><td>30. (A)</td><td></td><td></td><td></td><td></td><td></td></tr>
</table>

HOTS (ACHIEVERS SECTION)

31. (D)	32. (C)	33. (C)	34. (B)	35. (C)

34. (B) as you and him are representing people.

35. (C) as ours show possession.

4. VERBS

Answer Key

<table>
<tr><td colspan="5" align="center">I</td></tr>
<tr><td>1. Sung</td><td>2. Cost</td><td>3. Won</td><td>4. Seen</td><td>5. Flew</td></tr>
<tr><td>6. Became</td><td>7. Cut</td><td>8. Written</td><td>9. Built</td><td>10. Chosen</td></tr>
<tr><td>11. Gave, saw</td><td>12. Spent</td><td>13. Understood</td><td>14. Taken</td><td>15. Knew</td></tr>
<tr><td colspan="5" align="center">II</td></tr>
<tr><td>16. Showed</td><td>17. Eaten</td><td>18. Shrunk</td><td>19. Chose</td><td>20. Gone</td></tr>
<tr><td>21. Costs</td><td>22. Met</td><td>23. Heard</td><td>24. Torn</td><td>25. Caught</td></tr>
</table>

HOTS (ACHIEVERS SECTION)

31. (b)	32. (d)	33. (a)	34. (c)	35. (b)

Answer Key

I				
1. When	2. How	3. How much	4. Where	5. When
6. How	7. Where	8. When	9. How many	10. How many

II									
11. (B)	12. (B)	13. (A)	14. (B)	15. (A)	16. (B)	17. (A)	18. (A)	19. (A)	20. (B)
21. (B)	22. (B)	23. (A)	24. (B)	25. (A)	26. (A)	27. (A)	28. (A)	29. (B)	30. (B)

HOTS (ACHIEVERS SECTION)

31. At 11	32. Assam	33. Partially agree	34. (a)	35. (a)

6. ARTICLES AND PREPOSITIONS

Answer Key

I									
1. (A)	2. (D)	3. (A)	4. (B)	5. (B)	6. (D)	7. (A)	8. (B)	9. (B)	10. (B)
11. (B)	12. (B)	13. (A)	14. (B)	15. (B)					

II									
16. On	17. In	18. On	19. On	20. In	21. In	22. At	23. In	24. On	25. At

HOTS (ACHIEVERS SECTION)

26. (B)	27. (B)	28. (B)	29. (C)	30. (C)

I. Once upon a time, there lived an ant and a grasshopper in a grassy meadow. It was during the hot summer season when the ant was toiling hard by collecting wheat grains from the farmer's field. On the other hand, the grasshopper spent all his time in singing and dancing. He would frequently call the ant to join him in singing and dancing. However, the ant would ignore him and continue with her work. The ant said that she was saving some food for the cold season and recommended <u>the</u> grasshopper to follow <u>the</u> same. <u>The</u> grasshopper didn't pay heed to her words and continued singing and dancing merrily. Soon summer faded to autumn and autumn to winter. Out of cold, <u>the</u> grasshopper lost his interest in singing and making merry. He was cold and hungry and had no place to take shelter from <u>the</u> snow outside. Suddenly he remembered about <u>the</u> ant and visited her for some food and shelter. <u>The</u> grasshopper made <u>an</u> approach to her for some food and shelter. She gently asked him to sing somewhere else and earn his food and shelter. It is then, <u>the</u> grasshopper realized that he should have saved up enough for <u>the</u> winter instead of wasting his time being lazy during summer in singing and dancing around.

II. Gautam Buddha was born <u>in</u> 563 BC <u>at</u> Lumbini <u>in</u> Sakya Kshatriya clan <u>of</u> Kapilvastu <u>on</u> Vaiskha Purnima Day. His father Suddhodhana was the Saka ruler, his mother Mahamaya died <u>after</u> 7 days <u>of</u> his birth, so he was brought up <u>by</u> stepmother Gautami. He left home <u>at</u> the age <u>of</u> 29 years. He attained enlightenment <u>at</u> 35 years <u>of</u> age <u>at</u> Bodh Gaya <u>under</u> a pipal tree <u>on</u> the banks <u>of</u> Phalgu river <u>on</u> the 49th day <u>of</u> meditation.

7. CONTRACTIONS AND CONJUNCTIONS

Answer Key

I

1. (B)	2. (A)	3. (C)	4. (A)	5. (C)	6. (A)	7. (B)	8. (B)	9. (B)	10. (A)
11. (C)	12. (A)	13. (B)	14. (C)	15. (B)					

II

16. (D)	17. (B)	18. (A)	19. (C)	20. (D)	21. (A)	22. (B)	23. (B)	24. (B)	25. (A)
26. (B)	27. (A)	28. (C)	29. (A)	30. (B)					

HOTS (ACHIEVERS SECTION)

31. (B)	32. (B)	33. (A)	34. (C)	35. (D)

8. TENSES

Answer Key

I.

1. Opens	2. Will call	3. Will spill over	4. Talked	5. Swim
6. Is	7. Says	8. Will take us	9. Is going to speak	10. Heated
11. Comes	12. Sailed	13. Will get	14. Am going to	15. Rings

<table>
<tr><td colspan="10" align="center">II.</td></tr>
<tr><td>16. (A)</td><td>17. (C)</td><td>18. (C)</td><td>19. (D)</td><td>20. (B)</td><td>21. (A)</td><td>22. (B)</td><td>23. (C)</td><td>24. (A)</td><td>25. (B)</td></tr>
<tr><td>26. (D)</td><td>27. (D)</td><td>28. (C)</td><td>29. (A)</td><td>30. (B)</td><td></td><td></td><td></td><td></td><td></td></tr>
</table>

HOTS (ACHIEVERS SECTION)

31. evaporates	32. gets	33. goes	34. condenses	35. go
36. comes	37. do you know	38. happens	39. does not seep	40. collects
41. rises	42. converts			

9. JUMBLE WORDS AND IDIOMS/PROVERBS

Answer Key

1. (A)	2. (C)	3. (B)	4. (C)	5. (D)	6. (C)	7. (B)	8. (B)	9. (B)	10. (A)
11. (B)	12. (D)	13. (B)	14. (C)	15. (C)	16. (C)	17. (A)	18. (A)	19. (D)	20. (A)

HOTS (ACHIEVERS SECTION)

1. (D)	2. (B)	3. (C)	4. (A)	5. (C)

10. ARTICLES

Answer Key

Comprehension 1

1. (a) Very joyful and content.

(b) Being completely different from each other.

(c) To be unhappy because someone has something that you want for yourself.

(d) You have to bear the consequences of your actions.

(e) To be healthy, strong and fit.

2. (a) Anand worked at a sugar factory.

(b) Yes, he liked working there because he liked eating sweets.

(c) No

(d) At Anand's house.

(e) Anand used to save grains for the winters.

(f) Gautam went to the king of the jungle, the lion to complain.

(g) Gautam told the king that there should be a law to ensure everybody gets food when hungry.

(h) No

(i) The king told Gautam that he can't take fruits of labour away from Anand.

(j) We should work hard to secure our future otherwise we will reap what we sow.

Comprehension 2

3. It was Revathy's birthday.

4. Anish couldn't go to Revathy's birthday party because he was busy with cricket practice.

5. Yes, the team has a good chance of in the Zonal finals.

6. For three years.

7. Yes, Gopal did go to Revathy's party.

8. The kids went paintball shooting in the afternoon.

9. The kids went to McDonald's for lunch.

10. No, Anish has never been paint balling.

11. To an outlet in sector-18.

12. For two hours.

13. Revathy and Aisha were captains of two teams respectively.

14. Revathy and has team won the paint-ball competition.

15. Little toys that come with happy meal at McDonald's.

16. Yes.

17. At the McDonald's.

18. Rohan won the first round.

19. The clown made the kids laugh a lot.

20. The magician made a rabbit disappear and showed a mile-long handkerchief.

21. The gymnasts swaying on the trapeze looked like hanging from the sky.

22. Anish and Gopal saw the highlights of the football match that was played the night before.

Answer Key

I.

1. Introduction	2. Accepting request	3. Apology
4. Greeting	5. Accepting apology	6. Introduction
7. Accepting apology	8. Responding to requeat	9. Accepting apology
10. Greeting	11. Introduction	12. Responding to request
13. Apology	14. Greeting	15. Accepting apology

II.

16. (A)	17. (C)	18. (B)	19. (A)	20. (B)	21. (C)	22. (A)	23. (C)	24. (B)	25. (C)

MODEL TEST PAPER

Answer Key

I.

1. (A)	2. (D)	3. (C)	4. (B)	5. (B)	6. (A)	7. (D)	8. (C)	9. (B)	10. (A)
11. (B)	12. (A)	13. (B)	14. (A)	15. (D)	16. (D)	17. (B)	18. (A)	19. (C)	20. (B)

II.

21. (A)	22. (B)	23. (B)	24. (A)	25. (C)	26. (B)	27. (A)	28. (A)	29. (C)	30. (D)

III.

31 (A)	32. (C)	33. (C)	34. (B)	35. (D)					

SAMPLE OMR ANSWER SHEET

1. STUDENT NAME (IN ENGLISH CAPITAL LETTERS ONLY)

Students must write and darken the respective circles completely using HB Pencil only. Othewise their Answer Sheets will not be evaluated.

PERSONAL DETAILS

2. SCHOOL CODE

3. CLASS

4. SECTION

5. ROLL NO.

6. QUESTION PAPER SET

A ◯   B ◯   C ◯   D ◯

7. MOBILE NUMBER

8. GENDER

MALE ◯

FEMALE ◯

9. STREAM
(Only for Class XI and XII Students)

MATHEMATICS ◯
BIOLOGY ◯
OTHERS ◯

MARK YOUR ANSWERS

No.	A	B	C	D		No.	A	B	C	D
1.	Ⓐ	Ⓑ	Ⓒ	Ⓓ		26.	Ⓐ	Ⓑ	Ⓒ	Ⓓ
2.	Ⓐ	Ⓑ	Ⓒ	Ⓓ		27.	Ⓐ	Ⓑ	Ⓒ	Ⓓ
3.	Ⓐ	Ⓑ	Ⓒ	Ⓓ		28.	Ⓐ	Ⓑ	Ⓒ	Ⓓ
4.	Ⓐ	Ⓑ	Ⓒ	Ⓓ		29.	Ⓐ	Ⓑ	Ⓒ	Ⓓ
5.	Ⓐ	Ⓑ	Ⓒ	Ⓓ		30.	Ⓐ	Ⓑ	Ⓒ	Ⓓ
6.	Ⓐ	Ⓑ	Ⓒ	Ⓓ		31.	Ⓐ	Ⓑ	Ⓒ	Ⓓ
7.	Ⓐ	Ⓑ	Ⓒ	Ⓓ		32.	Ⓐ	Ⓑ	Ⓒ	Ⓓ
8.	Ⓐ	Ⓑ	Ⓒ	Ⓓ		33.	Ⓐ	Ⓑ	Ⓒ	Ⓓ
9.	Ⓐ	Ⓑ	Ⓒ	Ⓓ		34.	Ⓐ	Ⓑ	Ⓒ	Ⓓ
10.	Ⓐ	Ⓑ	Ⓒ	Ⓓ		35.	Ⓐ	Ⓑ	Ⓒ	Ⓓ
11.	Ⓐ	Ⓑ	Ⓒ	Ⓓ		36.	Ⓐ	Ⓑ	Ⓒ	Ⓓ
12.	Ⓐ	Ⓑ	Ⓒ	Ⓓ		37.	Ⓐ	Ⓑ	Ⓒ	Ⓓ
13.	Ⓐ	Ⓑ	Ⓒ	Ⓓ		38.	Ⓐ	Ⓑ	Ⓒ	Ⓓ
14.	Ⓐ	Ⓑ	Ⓒ	Ⓓ		39.	Ⓐ	Ⓑ	Ⓒ	Ⓓ
15.	Ⓐ	Ⓑ	Ⓒ	Ⓓ		40.	Ⓐ	Ⓑ	Ⓒ	Ⓓ
16.	Ⓐ	Ⓑ	Ⓒ	Ⓓ		41.	Ⓐ	Ⓑ	Ⓒ	Ⓓ
17.	Ⓐ	Ⓑ	Ⓒ	Ⓓ		42.	Ⓐ	Ⓑ	Ⓒ	Ⓓ
18.	Ⓐ	Ⓑ	Ⓒ	Ⓓ		43.	Ⓐ	Ⓑ	Ⓒ	Ⓓ
19.	Ⓐ	Ⓑ	Ⓒ	Ⓓ		44.	Ⓐ	Ⓑ	Ⓒ	Ⓓ
20.	Ⓐ	Ⓑ	Ⓒ	Ⓓ		45.	Ⓐ	Ⓑ	Ⓒ	Ⓓ
21.	Ⓐ	Ⓑ	Ⓒ	Ⓓ		46.	Ⓐ	Ⓑ	Ⓒ	Ⓓ
22.	Ⓐ	Ⓑ	Ⓒ	Ⓓ		47.	Ⓐ	Ⓑ	Ⓒ	Ⓓ
23.	Ⓐ	Ⓑ	Ⓒ	Ⓓ		48.	Ⓐ	Ⓑ	Ⓒ	Ⓓ
24.	Ⓐ	Ⓑ	Ⓒ	Ⓓ		49.	Ⓐ	Ⓑ	Ⓒ	Ⓓ
25.	Ⓐ	Ⓑ	Ⓒ	Ⓓ		50.	Ⓐ	Ⓑ	Ⓒ	Ⓓ

Signature of the Student & Date of Examination

Signature of the Invigilator & Date of Examination

V&S Publishers, F-2/16 Ansari Road, Daryaganj, New Delhi-110002, ☎ 011-23240026-27
✉ info@vspublishers.com, ⊕ www.vspublishers.com